The Uncharted Years

The Uncharted Years

Why You Feel Behind

By Carol Anne Harrison

Safe Harbor Collective™

THE UNCHARTED YEARS

Third Edition

Published by Safe Harbor Collective™

Galveston, Texas www.safeharborcollective.com

This book is a work of nonfiction. The events, conversations, and experiences detailed within reflect the creator's personal recollections. Some names and identifying details have been changed to protect privacy.

For permissions, inquiries, or more information, please contact:

Safe Harbor Collective™ www.safeharborcollective.com

ISBN: 979-8-90656-001-8 (paperback)
ISBN: 979-8-90656-002-5 (hardcover)
ISBN: 979-8-90656-000-1 (ebook)

Printed in the United States of America

If you or someone you know is struggling, you can call or text 988 for the Suicide & Crisis Lifeline. It is free, confidential, and available 24/7.

To my daughters.

I wish I would have had these words when you were younger.

And to anyone who feels lost and alone...

may these pages remind you that you are right where you need

to be.

Contents

Preface

I didn't write this book from a distance. I wrote it from the middle of the fog. From the years when I felt behind. From the seasons when I didn't recognize myself. From the moments when the map I thought I was supposed to follow dissolved in my hands.

I wrote it from the quiet rebuilds, the identity earthquakes, the emotional weather: the detours, the panic, the pressure, the becoming. I wrote it from the uncharted places no one prepares you for.

If you're holding this book, you might be in one of those places too. Maybe you feel lost. Maybe you feel late. Maybe you feel like everyone else got a map you somehow missed. Maybe you're trying to figure out who you are, or who you're becoming, or how to take the next step when you can't see the path.

If so, I want you to know something I wish someone had told me:

You are not behind.

You are not broken.

You are not the only one who feels this way.

You are in your uncharted years... the years when everything feels uncertain, shifting, unfinished.

The years when you're rebuilding yourself from the inside out. The years when you're learning to trust your own voice, your own pace, your own direction. These years are not a detour.

They are the path.

This book isn't a map. It's a companion. A place to rest. A place to breathe. A place to feel seen in the parts of your life that don't have language yet.

I wrote it for the version of me who needed someone to sit beside her and say, "You're not lost. You're becoming." And I wrote it for you... wherever you are, whatever season you're in, whatever pieces you're carrying.

You don't need to have it all figured out. You don't need to know the destination. You don't need to move faster than your body or your heart can go. You need a compass. And you're already building one.

Welcome to The Uncharted Years.

I'm honored to walk with you.

Introduction

You're Not Supposed to Know Yet

There's a quiet panic that lives inside early adulthood. A pressure to know who you are, where you're going, and how to get there before you've even had the chance to live enough life to figure it out.

You're told to choose a path. Pick a major. Pick a career. Pick a future. Pick a version of yourself and commit to it.

But how do you choose a direction when you don't even know your own internal landscape yet?

How do you build a life when you're still learning who you are beneath the expectations, the pressure, the noise?

No one tells you that you're not supposed to know yet, that uncertainty is normal, that feeling lost is part of the process, or that the uncharted years aren't a mistake. They're a season.

This book exists because I needed someone to tell me those things.

And because you might need someone to tell you too.

What This Book Is

This book is a companion for the years when everything feels uncertain, shifting, unfinished. It's a guide for the seasons when you're rebuilding yourself from the inside out. It's a place to rest when you're overwhelmed by the pressure to have it all figured out.

It's not a map. It's not a checklist. It's not a set of rules. It's a compass. One you'll build as you move through these pages.

You'll see the word becoming throughout these pages. I use it intentionally because becoming isn't one destination. It's the lifelong process of growing into the person you choose to be. For one person, becoming might mean finding courage. For another, it might mean finding peace, setting boundaries, healing old wounds, or finally trusting themselves. There is no single definition because your journey of becoming belongs to you.

What This Book Is Not

This book won't tell you who to be. It won't tell you what path to choose. It won't promise clarity on a timeline. It won't pretend that becoming is easy, linear, or fast.

Instead, it will help you understand the emotional terrain of early adulthood: the fog, the storms, the droughts, the sun breaks. It will help you recognize the internal shifts that signal growth. It will help you rebuild gently after the identity earthquakes. It will help you trust your own pace, your own voice, your own direction.

Why You Might Feel Lost

You're not lost because you're failing. You're lost because you're becoming. You're shedding old versions of yourself, and questioning inherited beliefs. You're learning what feels true, while building boundaries. You're discovering your values, and navigating emotional weather you've never experienced before.

Feeling lost is not a flaw. It's a sign that you're in motion.

How to Use This Book

You don't have to read it in order. You don't have to take notes. You don't have to treat it like homework.

Move through it the way you move through your own becoming; slowly, gently, honestly. Pause when something resonates. Return to chapters when you need them. Skip ahead when your heart pulls you forward.

This book is not meant to be rushed through. It's meant to be lived with.

A Final Word Before We Begin

You don't need to know the destination. You don't need to have a plan. You don't need to rush. You need to take the next honest step.

The Uncharted Years are not a detour. They are the path.

Let's walk it together.

Chapter 1

The Myth of the Correct Route

The Feeling No One Warned You About

No one tells you that adulthood doesn't start with excitement.

It starts with this quiet, sinking feeling.

You're scrolling, listening, watching, and there it is again. Someone you know posted something big like a new apartment or a college acceptance, a job announcement with a caption that sounds effortless.

You close the browser, the book, the conversation, and stare at the ceiling.

And the thought shows upright on time:

I'm behind.

Not failing. Not lazy. Just late. Like you missed a turn somewhere and everyone else kept going without you.

That feeling isn't a personal flaw. It's a response to a lie you were handed. The lie says adulthood is supposed to feel like a launch. Like fireworks. Like a race where everyone takes off at the same time.

But the reality is quieter. It's slower and oftentimes messier. And when you realize that, the sinking feeling starts to make sense. You're not broken. You're not late. You're standing at the edge of a story that doesn't match the one you were told.

Running Ahead, Still Behind

At sixteen, I thought graduating early would prove I was ahead. A scholarship dangled in front of me, $1,000, which felt enormous at that age, and I couldn't resist. I doubled up, taking my junior and senior year together, and walked across the stage a few months before turning seventeen.

But even as I held the diploma, the panic was already there. I remembered sitting in a college-prep meeting where the seniors were told that we should have been applying to colleges our junior year. I was already behind. Why hadn't anyone told me sooner?

I enrolled at the closest junior college, signed up for basics, and landed in remedial math and writing. Those placement tests felt like a verdict: proof that I wasn't ready, proof that I didn't belong. Nothing felt right. I felt like a fake, like I was pretending to belong in a place that didn't fit me.

I finished a year, then transferred to the junior college most of my original graduating class had gone to. It was their first year, and I felt behind. I was eighteen, clueless about what I wanted, and exhausted from trying to catch up.

I dropped out after a few weeks. Cosmetology seemed like a quick fix. I became a nail tech, had a trade, something that would get me into the "real world" workforce. I didn't like it, but I pushed through. I did all these things because I thought it was what I was supposed to do. I didn't want to disappoint my family. I didn't want to be a failure.

At nineteen, I moved out with a friend, desperate to prove independence. Bills piled up, sadness deepened, and eventually I had to move back in with my parents. Every move felt like a step backward, even though I was trying so hard to step forward.

By twenty, I was seeing someone willing to marry me. And that was enough. I wanted to start my adult life, to prove I was on track. Hindsight is 20/20. I see now that every choice was shaped by the myth, by the pressure to be "on time," even when I was lost.

The Friend Who Looked "On Track"

She was the kind of person everyone pointed to as proof that the "correct route" worked. She was a straight-A student, varsity athlete, college acceptance letter pinned to the refrigerator with a smiley-face magnet.

From the outside, she was ahead. She was the model. She was the one we all compared ourselves to when we felt late.

But years later, she told me the truth.

She hated her major. She had chosen it because it sounded impressive, not because it fit her. Every lecture felt like a performance, every exam a test of endurance. She cried herself to sleep most nights, convinced she couldn't admit she was miserable because everyone had already invested in her success.

Her relationship looked perfect in the Polaroids taped to her dorm wall of homecoming dances, football games, and smiles that looked permanent. But behind closed doors, she felt trapped. She stayed because leaving would mean admitting the dream wasn't hers.

She was "on track," but she was suffocating.

The Global Contrast

While I was panicking about remedial classes and rushing into marriage, a friend of mine from another culture was living a completely different version of early adulthood.

She grew up in a household where staying home until marriage wasn't just accepted, it was expected.

At nineteen, she wasn't scrambling to prove independence. She wasn't rushing to rent an apartment or pick a major. She was living with her parents, contributing to the household, and saving money. In her family's eyes, that wasn't failure. It was normal.

When I told her I felt "behind," she looked at me with confusion. Behind what?

Her timeline was slower, but it wasn't shameful. It was respected.

That contrast taught me something I couldn't see at the time: the "correct route" is not universal. Sometimes it's cultural.

The Empty Success Story

He did everything right.

Graduated on time, went straight to a four-year university, picked a practical major, landed an internship, secured a job before graduation.

From the outside, he was the myth made flesh. But when I sat across from him years later, he said quietly, "I don't even know who I am."

He had followed the route so faithfully that he never stopped to ask if it fit him. His degree was chosen for stability, not passion. His job was chosen for security, not joy. His relationship was chosen for timing, not readiness.

He wasn't behind. He wasn't late. He wasn't failing.

He was empty.

The Gap Year Student

She didn't go straight to college. Instead, she worked at a coffee shop, saved money, and traveled with friends. Everyone around her whispered that she was "falling behind." Relatives asked when she would "get serious." Teachers shook their heads, disappointed that she hadn't "used her potential."

But during that year, she learned resilience. She woke up at 5

a.m. to open the café, learned how to manage difficult customers, and discovered the quiet pride of paying her own bills. She learned how to budget, how to navigate airports, how to meet strangers and build friendships across cultures. She learned how to sit in silence on a train in a foreign country and realize she was capable of being alone without being lonely.

Her peers were rushing through dorm life, cramming for exams, and posting photos of campus events. She was learning how to cook simple meals, how to negotiate rent with a landlord, how to stretch $20 across three days. She was learning adulthood in real time.

When she finally enrolled in school, she carried confidence her peers didn't have. She wasn't late. She was layered. Her detour gave her depth, and that depth became her compass.

The Career Pivoter

He followed the route: degree, internship, job. On paper, he was perfect with an impressive resume, a stable salary, and a life that seemed enviable. But five years in, he realized he was miserable. Every morning, he sat in traffic with a knot in his stomach. Every evening, he came home drained, staring at the ceiling, wondering if this was all life had to offer.

He left his stable career to pursue art. Everyone said he was reckless. His parents worried. His colleagues whispered. His friends told him he was throwing away security. But he said, "I'd rather be late to joy than early to emptiness."

The pivot wasn't easy. He worked odd jobs to pay rent. He faced rejection after rejection. He questioned himself constantly. But he also felt alive. He painted until midnight, lost track of time in the studio, and rediscovered the thrill of creating something that mattered to him.

His detour wasn't failure. It was survival. It was the choice to honor his own compass instead of a map that didn't fit. Years later, when his art began to sell, people called him brave. But bravery wasn't the point. The point was that he had chosen to live.

The Mental Health Detour

She paused school for therapy. She paused work for recovery.

She carried shame for years, convinced she had "fallen behind." Friends graduated. Siblings moved out. Social media filled with announcements of promotions, engagements, and milestones. She sat in waiting rooms, filled out intake forms, and wondered if anyone else felt as broken as she did.

But therapy taught her language for her pain. Recovery taught her patience with her body. She learned how to breathe through panic, how to name her triggers, how to ask for help without apology. She learned that healing was not weakness. It was work.

When she returned, she was stronger, steadier, and more self-aware than anyone around her. She could sit with discomfort. She could hold boundaries. She could recognize when urgency was the myth speaking, not her truth.

Her detour wasn't weakness. It was wisdom. It was the choice to pause instead of collapse. It was the recognition that becoming sometimes requires stopping, resting, and rebuilding before moving forward.

The Hidden Cost of the Myth

These stories, mine, hers, his, reveal the same truth:

The myth doesn't just wound those who feel behind. It wounds those who feel forced to stay ahead.

The myth traps both sides: those who feel late carry shame, and those who feel ahead carry pressure. Both are lost. Both are hurting. Both are navigating waters that don't fit their compass.

For those who feel late, the cost is internalized shame. Every detour feels like proof of failure. Every pause feels like wasted time. They replay timelines in their heads, measuring themselves against classmates, coworkers, siblings, and strangers online. The myth whispers: You're too slow. You missed your chance. You'll never catch up.

For those who feel ahead, the cost is silent pressure. Every achievement becomes a cage. They can't admit they're unhappy without disappointing everyone who believed in their route. They can't change direction without fearing they'll lose their place in line. The myth whispers: Don't stop. Don't question.

Don't let anyone down.

The shame of being late and the pressure of being ahead are two sides of the same coin. Both silence the truth. Both erase the possibility of choosing differently. Both keep young adults locked in stories that don't fit.

And the hidden cost is this: the myth steals presence.

You can't enjoy where you are because you're haunted by where you think you should be. You can't celebrate your progress because you're terrified of losing momentum. You can't rest because you're convinced rest equals failure.

The myth convinces you adulthood is a race. But races have winners and losers. Life doesn't.

Why the "Correct Route" Became a Myth

The "correct route" didn't appear out of nowhere. It was built under specific historical conditions such as post-war prosperity, industrial sequencing, rigid gender roles, and a booming economy that made linear adulthood possible.

In the 1950s and 1960s, adulthood was scripted like a factory line: graduate high school, attend college or enter the workforce, marry young, buy a house, start a family, retire after 30 years of stable employment. The economy supported this sequence. Wages were high enough to buy homes in your twenties. College tuition was affordable. Jobs were plentiful and often lifelong. The myth of the "correct route" was not just cultural; it was structural.

But those conditions no longer exist.

Generational Shifts

Boomers grew up with stability. Their adulthood was linear, predictable, and supported by policy.

Gen X began to see cracks: layoffs, rising divorce rates, shifting gender roles.

Millennials inherited debt, housing crises, and a gig economy that reshaped adulthood. Their adulthood became nonlinear by necessity.

Gen Z entered adulthood in the shadow of climate anxiety, social media comparison, and economic precarity.

The myth remains, but the scaffolding that held it up has collapsed. Young adults are told to follow a route that no longer exists.

The Role of Social Media

Social media accelerates comparison. In earlier generations, you compared yourself to neighbors or classmates. Now, you compare yourself to thousands of curated timelines.

Instagram shows highlight reels of "success."

LinkedIn celebrates promotions and career milestones.

TikTok glamorizes lifestyles that are unattainable for most.

The myth whispers louder online: You're late. You're missing out. You're not enough.

But what social media doesn't show are the detours, the pauses, the breakdowns, the therapy sessions, the nights of doubt. The myth thrives on silence; on the absence of stories that reveal nonlinear paths.

Economic Realities

The myth assumes stability. But stability has eroded.

Student debt delays independence.

Housing costs push adulthood milestones further out.

Gig work replaces long-term careers with short contracts.

Healthcare costs make risk-taking harder.

The myth punishes deviation, but deviation is now the norm.

Most young adults are navigating conditions that make the "correct route" impossible.

Global Contrasts

In some cultures, adulthood is slower, communal, and differently sequenced.

In parts of Asia, living with parents until marriage is expected; not shameful.

In Mediterranean cultures, adulthood is often extended, with family support lasting well into the thirties.

In Indigenous communities, adulthood is defined less by milestones and more by contribution to the collective.

The myth of the "correct route" is not universal. It is cultural and deeply Western. Recognizing this contrast helps dismantle the shame.

Toolkit: Naming Your Route

Here are twelve practices to help you reclaim authorship of your adulthood:

Timeline Trap

Write the "correct route" you absorbed vs. your actual route. Circle divergences. Why this matters: It helps you see where the myth is shaping your panic.

Whose Map Is It?

List the voices behind your expectations. Why this matters: It shows you whose pressure you're carrying.

Reframing Divergence

For each divergence, name one strength it gave you. Why this matters: It reframes detours as growth, not failure. Myth Detector

When panic hits, ask this: Is this urgency mine or the myth's? Why this matters: It helps you separate your truth from cultural noise.

Global Compass Mapping

Compare your cultural expectations to other cultures. Why this matters: It reminds you there is no single timeline.

Comparison Detox

Track your social media triggers for one week. Why this matters: It reveals how often the myth sneaks in through curated timelines.

Detour Strengths Map

Write three skills you gained from each detour. Why this matters: It shifts focus from what you "lost" to what you built. Compass Journaling

Each day, write: "What feels true today?" Why this matters:

It builds trust in your own voice and not external timelines. Timeline Rewrite

Draft your own adulthood sequence, free from cultural myths.

Why this matters: It gives you authorship over your story.

Anchor Practice

Choose one word to describe your current season. Place it somewhere visible. Why this matters: Naming anchors you in presence.

Permission Slip

Write yourself a note: "I am allowed to be in a season that doesn't look like anyone else's." Why this matters: It externalizes permission and softens shame.

Compass Conversation

Share your season name with a trusted friend. Why this matters: Saying it aloud reduces shame and invites support.

Closing Compass Point

There is no single correct route. There are only routes that fit the conditions of your harbor, the winds of your season, and the compass of your values. Once you name the myth, you can begin to release it and chart your own route.

You are not broken. You are not late. You are not failing.

You are in your Uncharted Years.

And once you identify them, you can begin to chart them.

Chapter 2

The Uncharted Years Defined

Naming the Season

This book exists because early adulthood has no socially recognized season.

When I was nineteen, I didn't have words for what I was going through. I only had feelings: panic, shame, confusion, exhaustion. I thought being "out of order" meant I had failed. I thought the detours were proof that I had ruined something important; that I had broken the sequence everyone else seemed to follow so naturally.

But then I stumbled into a realization: maybe it wasn't failure. Maybe it was simply different.

That's when the phrase came to me: The Uncharted Years.

They were seasons without a prescribed charter, without anyone authorizing my becoming. Messy, nonlinear, full of detours. And yet, they were mine.

Naming them didn't fix everything, but it gave me a compass.

It permitted me to stop calling myself broken.

Out of Order, Not Failure

At twenty-one, I was married and pregnant. I wasn't ready for school. I wasn't ready for adulthood in the way the myth had scripted it. My choices felt "out of order."

Everywhere I looked, the sequence seemed clear: finish college, start a career, build independence, then think about marriage and family. My life didn't match that script. I was skipping steps, rearranging milestones, living a timeline that felt upside-down.

The shame was heavy. I thought I had ruined something important, that I had broken the invisible rules everyone else seemed to follow. But slowly, I began to realize: "out of order" wasn't the same as "wrong." It was simply my order.

That shift, from shame to naming, changed everything. Naming permitted me to see my life as a story, not a mistake. It allowed me to hold both truths at once: that my path was different, and that different could still be valid.

When I reframed my choices as my order, I stopped measuring myself against someone else's map. I began to see the strengths hidden in the detours: resilience, adaptability, courage. My order was uncharted, but it was mine.

The Client Who Named Her Season

A young woman once told me she felt like she was "late to life." She hadn't gone to college, hadn't moved out, hadn't checked the boxes she thought she was supposed to. Every conversation with friends reminded her of what she hadn't done. Every family gathering carried questions she didn't know how to answer.

She carried the word failure like a shadow. It followed her into job interviews, into relationships, into quiet nights alone.

She believed she had missed her chance.

I asked her, "What would you call this season if you didn't call it failure?"

She paused. The silence stretched. Then she said, "My rebuilding years."

The relief on her face was immediate. Her shoulders dropped. Her breath deepened. Naming her season didn't erase the struggle, but it reframed it. It gave her a story that wasn't shame.

From that moment, she began to see her choices differently.

Staying home wasn't proof of failure; it was rebuilding stability. Working part-time wasn't falling behind; it was laying groundwork. Her detours became chapters, not verdicts.

Naming gave her agency. It allowed her to step out of comparison and into authorship. And that shift, from shame to naming, is what transforms the Uncharted Years from a fog into a compass.

Why Naming Matters

Naming is more than semantics. It's survival.

Naming externalizes shame

When you name the season, you move shame outside yourself. It becomes something you're in, not something you are.

Naming protects identity

Without a name, detours become identity statements.

- "I failed."
- "I'm behind."
- "I'm not enough."

With a name, the narrative shifts:

- "I'm in my Uncharted Years."
- "I'm in a rebuilding season."
- "I'm in a learning chapter."

Naming restores agency

When you name your season, you reclaim authorship. You stop living someone else's map and start writing your own.

Cultures name adolescence, midlife, retirement, but early adulthood has been left unnamed, except for the myth of the

"correct route." That silence breeds shame. Naming fills the gap.

Naming is not about erasing struggle. It's about reframing it. It's about giving yourself language that softens the weight and restores perspective.

The Universal Shadow

I've seen this shadow across ages:

- A twenty-year-old who feels late to college.
- A twenty-five-year-old who feels late to marriage.
- A thirty-year-old who feels late to career.

Different ages, same shadow.

The shadow whispers: You're late. You missed your chance. You'll never catch up.

But when they name their season, "my learning years," "my healing years," "my Uncharted Years," the shadow lifts. Their shoulders drop. Their breath deepens. Their story softens.

Naming doesn't erase the fog, but it gives you a compass. It allows you to walk through the shadow with language that reminds you: this is a season, not a sentence.

The Moment I Realized My Life Was Different

Let me preface this with the truth: I love my daughters. I am grateful for them, and I wouldn't undo their existence for anything. But loving them doesn't erase what those early years felt like. Love and grief can coexist. Gratitude and ache can share the same room.

When I was married and pregnant, I would watch my friends go out and have fun; piling into cars, getting dressed up, laughing about plans that didn't require permission or planning. They were living the version of early adulthood I thought I was supposed to have. The version I had imagined for myself before life took a sharp turn.

I remember one night in particular. I was sitting on the edge of my bed, the window cracked open just enough to let in the humid Texas air. Somewhere down the street, music drifted through the night: muffled bass, bursts of laughter, the sound of a door slamming as someone shouted, "Hurry up!" My friends were there. I could picture them clearly: hair curled, lip gloss shining, the thrill of possibility in their eyes.

I was home, exhausted, swollen, and trying to convince myself I wasn't missing anything. But I felt the ache anyway; the ache of knowing my life had shifted into a different season long before I was ready.

It wasn't regret.

It wasn't resentment.

It was grief for a version of myself I never got to be.

I didn't have the language for it then. I didn't know how to hold both truths at once: loving the life I had and mourning the life I didn't get to live. I didn't know that both could be real, both were valid, both could coexist without canceling each other out.

All I knew was that my friends were out there becoming, and I was becoming something else entirely: a wife, a mother, an adult long before I felt like one.

That was the moment I realized my life wasn't "out of order." It was simply different. And different didn't mean wrong.

Different meant unchartered.

The Parent Who Returned to School

At thirty-five, she walked into a classroom filled with twenty-year-olds. The desks felt too small, the chatter too fast, the references too foreign. She worried she would stand out, that everyone would notice she was older, slower, "late."

But she carried something her classmates didn't: years of lived experience. She had raised children, managed a household, worked jobs that demanded resilience. When the professor asked for examples, she could connect theory to practice in ways her peers couldn't.

At first, she felt embarrassed when classmates asked, "Why are you here?" But then she reframed it: I'm reclaiming. She wasn't late. She was reclaiming education, reclaiming dreams she had set aside, reclaiming a part of herself that had been waiting patiently.

Her season wasn't failure. It was reclamation. And naming it gave her courage to keep showing up, even when the textbooks felt heavy and the nights felt long.

The Entrepreneur Who Failed Forward

At twenty-seven, he launched a business with excitement and borrowed confidence. He rented an office, printed business cards, built a website. For a year, he poured everything into it: time, money, energy, hope.

And then it collapsed. Clients disappeared. Bills piled up. The dream dissolved. He carried shame like a second skin, convinced he had wasted his twenties.

But when he named the season "my learning years," the story shifted. Failure became foundation. Mistakes became lessons. He realized he had learned how to pitch, how to budget, how to adapt, how to survive disappointment.

Years later, when he launched a second business, those lessons became his scaffolding. The first collapse wasn't a waste of time. It was training. Naming it allowed him to see failure not as the end, but as the beginning of resilience.

The Artist Who Took a Pause

At twenty-four, she stopped painting. Her brushes sat in jars, her canvases gathered dust. She told herself she had lost her gift, that maybe she wasn't meant to be an artist after all.

But the truth was simpler: she was exhausted. She needed rest. She needed space. She needed to live without producing for a while.

Naming those two years as "my resting years" reframed the silence. Rest wasn't proof of failure. It was part of the process.

When she returned to painting, her work carried new depth: colors richer, strokes more intentional, themes more layered.

Her pause had given her perspective. Her resting years had become her renewal years.

Toolkit: Naming Practice

Here are six expanded exercises to help you name your season:

Write the Shame Script

What do you currently call this season? Late, behind, stuck, failing — write it down.

Reflection: How does it feel to see those words outside yourself?

Rewrite the Title

If this season were a book, what would its title be?

Examples: "My Rebuilding Years." "My Exploration Years."

"My Uncharted Years."

Anchor the Name

Place it somewhere visible: a mirror, a journal, your phone background.

Reflection: How does seeing it daily shift your perspective?

Share the Name

Tell a trusted friend: "I'm in my ___ years."

Reflection: Notice how saying it aloud changes the weight. Sometimes the simple act of naming aloud softens shame and invites support.

Season Mapping

Draw a timeline of your life so far. Mark the detours. Name each one.

Reflection: How does naming shift the story? What patterns emerge when you see your seasons laid out visually?

Permission Slip

Write yourself a note: "I am allowed to be in a season that doesn't look like anyone else's."

Reflection: How does giving yourself permission soften shame? Where in your body do you feel relief when you read it?

Closing Compass Point

Naming is the first act of reclamation. It doesn't erase the fog, but it gives you a compass.

You are not broken. You are not late. You are not failing.

You are in your Uncharted Years.

And once you name them, you can begin to navigate them.

Chapter 3

The Comparison Fog

The Fog Rolls In

Comparison doesn't arrive loudly. It doesn't knock on the door or announce itself with a trumpet blast. It drifts in quietly, like fog rolling across a harbor at dawn.

At first, the water is clear. You can see your own shoreline, your own compass, your own pace. Then, almost imperceptibly, the fog begins to thicken. It doesn't come all at once; it creeps in, soft and subtle, until suddenly you realize you can't see the horizon anymore.

One moment, your path feels steady. The next, it's blurred by someone else's timeline. Their milestones, their announcements, their curated images drift across your view, and you begin to wonder if you've taken a wrong turn.

Fog doesn't mean you're lost. It means your visibility is temporarily reduced. But when you don't know that, panic sets in. You start to believe the fog is truth. You start to believe you've lost your way.

Scrolling Through the Fog

At nineteen, I watched my peers post photos from dorm rooms, football games, study groups, and new friendships. They looked like they were stepping into the next chapter with confidence.

I felt like I was watching life happen from the outside.

I wasn't in a dorm. I wasn't choosing a major. I wasn't making new friends. I wasn't "becoming" in the way the world said I should be.

Every post felt like a reminder that I had taken a wrong turn. I didn't know then that I was comparing my behind-the-scenes to someone else's highlight reel.

Why Comparison Hits So Hard

Comparison today is heavier, faster, and constant.

Visibility: You see everything.

Curation: You see only the polished parts.

Pace: You see updates instantly.

Comparison used to be a whisper. Now it's a hum.

The Psychology of Comparison

Your brain interprets someone else's success as danger, as if it's a sign you're falling behind the group. It's primal, automatic, and not your fault.

Thousands of years ago, survival depended on staying with the tribe. If you fell behind, you risked being left vulnerable to predators, hunger, or isolation. The human nervous system learned to scan constantly: Am I keeping up? Am I safe? Am I still part of the group?

Back then, comparison was protective. It was a survival tool. If someone in the tribe learned to hunt faster, you paid attention. If someone discovered fire, you copied them. If someone built shelter, you followed their lead. Falling behind wasn't just inconvenient: it was life-threatening.

Today, the tribe is digital. The milestones are virtual. The predators are gone, but the instinct remains. Your brain still reacts as if being "behind" is dangerous. When you see someone post about a promotion, a wedding, a new house, or a vacation, your nervous system interprets it as a survival signal: They are ahead. You are at risk.

Comparison is wired into survival instincts. But in modern life, it misfires. Instead of protecting you, it punishes you. It tells you you're unsafe when you're simply different.

That's why comparison feels so visceral. It's not just a thought; it's a body reaction. Your chest tightens. Your stomach drops. Your pulse quickens. You feel the same physiological alarm bells that once warned your ancestors of danger.

But here's the truth: you are not in danger. You are not being left behind by a tribe that will abandon you. You are living in a world where timelines are diverse, nonlinear, and deeply personal. The fog convinces you that difference equals danger, but difference is simply difference.

Comparison is not proof that you're failing. It's proof that you're human.

The Family Milestone Fog

At thirty, a woman scrolled through her feed and saw cousins posting baby announcements and new homes. Her timeline was filled with pastel nurseries, ultrasound photos, and smiling couples holding keys in front of freshly painted doors. Each caption carried words like "Our greatest blessing" or "Finally homeowners!"

From the outside, it looked like everyone was moving forward in perfect rhythm. The milestones seemed like proof of arrival, evidence of success. But beneath the surface, the reality was far more complicated.

At a family gathering one summer, the living room was crowded with relatives passing a newborn from arm to arm. The baby wore a tiny knit cap, and the air was thick with laughter, congratulations, and the smell of casseroles warming in the oven. Cameras flashed, grandparents beamed, and the new parents smiled for every photo.

Later, in the quiet of the kitchen, away from the noise, the new mother leaned against the counter. Her smile faded as she whispered to her sister, "I cry almost every night. The postpartum depression is heavier than I thought it would be. I post the happy moments because I don't want anyone to worry."

Her words carried the weight of exhaustion. The fog had made her life look effortless, but the truth was layered with struggle.

In another corner of the family, a cousin had just bought a house. The photos online showed a couple standing proudly in front of a two-story home, the lawn freshly mowed, the caption reading: "Dreams do come true." At the gathering, relatives praised them for "getting ahead" and "building stability."

But over coffee, the cousin admitted quietly, "We're drowning in bills. The mortgage is bigger than we expected. Sometimes I wonder if we made a mistake."

Their milestones weren't the whole story. The fog had hidden their humanity. What looked like certainty was layered with exhaustion, doubt, and fear.

The Creative Fog

At twenty-four, a young writer sat at her desk surrounded by stacks of notebooks and half-finished drafts. The glow of her laptop screen illuminated the mess of sentences she had been wrestling with for weeks. Pages spilled across the floor, some scribbled with ideas, others abandoned mid-paragraph. She compared her unfinished manuscript to a friend's published book, the glossy cover smiling back at her from social media posts.

Her friend's book launch looked effortless. Photos showed her standing at a podium, signing copies for eager readers, smiling with stacks of her work beside her. The captions read: "So grateful for this journey." "Living my best life." The comments poured in: "You're amazing!" "Such an inspiration!"

The young writer stared at her own scattered drafts and thought: She's ahead. She's more talented. She's more disciplined. I'm failing.

Her own process felt messy, slow, and invisible. There were no launch parties for unfinished chapters, no applause for late nights spent deleting more words than she kept. She wondered if her pace meant she wasn't cut out for the work.

Years later, the two friends sat together in a café, their lives having unfolded in different directions. The published author stirred her coffee slowly, her eyes tired. "I rushed the book," she admitted. "I regret parts of it. I wish I had taken more time. Honestly, I envy your slower, more intentional pace. You're building something with depth. I sprinted, and now I feel trapped in what I published."

The confession startled the young writer. The fog had distorted both of their truths. One felt behind, the other felt trapped.

The Body Image Fog

Scrolling through fitness posts late at night, a young woman felt her chest tighten. The glow of her phone lit up the dark room as she swiped past photo after photo: toned bodies, glowing smiles, captions promising discipline, joy, and transformation. "Strong not skinny." "No excuses." "Best shape of my life."

Her own reflection in the mirror earlier that day had felt ordinary, unremarkable. She compared her quiet routines - a walk around the block, cooking simple meals, stretching before bed - to the polished images flooding her feed. Each post seemed to shout that she wasn't enough.

The fog whispered: They are happier. They are healthier.

They are stronger. You are failing.

But behind the camera, the truth was far more complicated.

One influencer, whose smile radiated confidence in every post, later admitted in an interview that she had been skipping meals, obsessively tracking calories, and battling shame in silence. Another confessed to exhaustion, saying, "I was working out twice a day, not because I loved it, but because I was terrified of losing followers."

The fog had turned pain into performance.

Her body wasn't proof of failure.

Their bodies weren't proof of joy. They were proof of pressure.

The Relationship Fog

At twenty-nine, a man scrolled through his feed and saw engagement photos everywhere. Rings glistened in close-up shots, couples posed in candlelit restaurants, and carefully staged proposals unfolded under twinkling lights. Captions read: "She said yes!" "Forever starts now."

From the outside, it looked effortless. Love, commitment, and joy all captured in a single frame. He stared at the photos and wondered if he was behind, if his single status was proof of failure.

The fog whispered: Everyone else has found their person.

You are alone. You are late.

At weddings, the pressure grew heavier. He sat at tables surrounded by couples, watching first dances and bouquet tosses, feeling like he was the only one still waiting. Relatives asked casually, "So, when will it be your turn?" Friends teased, "You're next!" Each question carried the weight of expectation, as if his timeline had expired.

But later, one friend admitted quietly, "I felt pressured into marriage. Everyone expected it. I wasn't sure, but I didn't want to disappoint anyone. The photos look happy, but I cry more than I thought I would."

Another confessed, "We rushed because everyone else was getting engaged. I didn't want to be the last one. Now I feel trapped in a commitment I wasn't ready for."

The fog had hidden their uncertainty. What looked like certainty was layered with doubt, fear, and pressure.

The Relationship Fog convinces us that love is a race, that timing is proof of worth, that milestones equal stability. But relationships aren't trophies. They are living, breathing commitments that require readiness, honesty, and choice.

His single status wasn't proof of failure. It was proof of discernment. It was proof that he was waiting for a connection that felt real, not one staged for photos.

The Academic Fog

At twenty-one, a student sat in the library scrolling through posts about scholarships, internships, and graduate school acceptances. Friends posed with acceptance letters, their faces glowing with pride. Captions read: "Off to Harvard!" "Thrilled to join this fellowship."

She looked down at her own rejection email and felt her stomach drop.

The fog whispered: They are smarter. They are ahead. You are falling behind.

The library around her hummed with the sound of pages turning, keyboards clicking, and whispered study groups. She stared at her laptop screen, the rejection letter glowing back at her, and felt the weight of silence pressing in. Every congratulatory post online seemed louder than the quiet of her own disappointment.

But what the posts didn't show were the sleepless nights, the anxiety attacks before exams, the quiet doubts about chosen majors. One friend admitted later, "I got the scholarship, but I'm terrified I won't live up to it. I feel like an imposter every day." Another confessed, "I post my wins because I don't want anyone to know how many times I cried in the bathroom before class."

The Academic Fog convinces students that grades and acceptances define worth. It hides the truth that learning is nonlinear, that intelligence is diverse, that success is not measured only by institutions.

She began to notice the hidden costs: classmates who looked polished but were drowning in debt, peers who posted about internships while secretly battling burnout, friends who smiled in graduation photos but felt hollow inside. The fog had turned achievement into performance, masking the humanity beneath.

Her rejection wasn't proof of failure. It was proof of redirection. The fog had told her she was behind, but she was simply on a different path; one that would teach resilience, adaptability, and the courage to define success on her own terms.

The Parenting Fog

Scrolling through social media, parents saw posts of children winning awards, playing sports, performing in recitals. Captions read: "So proud of my little genius!" "Future Olympian!" "She nailed her solo!"

One mother compared her child's quiet, introverted nature to the spotlight moments of others. She felt inadequate, as if her parenting had failed. Every scroll seemed to whisper: Other parents are raising stars. You are raising silence.

At a school assembly, she sat in the bleachers watching children line up for certificates. The gym echoed with applause, camera flashes, and the squeak of sneakers on polished floors. Parents leaned forward, phones raised high, capturing every moment. Her child sat quietly in the back row, hands folded, eyes down. No certificate. No spotlight. Just presence.

Her chest tightened. The fog whispered: You're not doing enough. You're not giving them what they need. You're failing.

Later that evening, another parent confided over coffee, "We post the wins because they're easy. What we don't post are the meltdowns, the sleepless nights, the therapy sessions. Behind every award photo is a week of struggle."

Another admitted, "My son looks confident on stage, but he cries every night before practice. We keep pushing because everyone expects him to shine. Sometimes I wonder if we're doing it for him or for us."

The Parenting Fog convinces parents that their children's achievements reflect their parenting. It hides the truth that love, patience, and presence matter more than trophies.

Her child's quietness wasn't proof of failure. It was proof of individuality. It was proof of a different rhythm; one that didn't need applause to be valid.

The Financial Fog

At thirty-five, a man scrolled through posts of friends buying new cars, remodeling kitchens, vacationing in Europe. Captions read: "Finally upgraded!" "Living the dream." "Worth every penny."

He looked around his modest apartment at the second-hand couch, the chipped coffee table, the hum of an old refrigerator, and felt small.

The fog whispered: They are successful. You are behind.

At dinner parties, the pressure grew heavier. Friends compared mortgage rates, debated renovation plans, and swapped stories about international travel. He smiled politely, stirring his drink, but inside he felt the ache of inadequacy. His quiet stability seemed invisible next to their glossy milestones.

Later, one friend admitted over a late-night phone call, "We're deep in debt. The car payment is crushing. The vacation went on a credit card we can't pay off. Honestly, I post the photos because I don't want anyone to know how scared I am."

Another confessed, "We remodeled the kitchen because everyone else was upgrading. But now we're juggling three jobs just to keep up with the bills. The photos look perfect, but the stress is unbearable."

The Financial Fog convinces us that possessions equal progress, that upgrades prove worth, that luxury is the measure of success. But behind the polished photos are often debt, anxiety, and sacrifice.

His modest apartment wasn't proof of failure. It was proof of sustainability. It was proof of living within his means, of choosing peace over pressure, of valuing stability over performance.

Years later, when many of his friends were still buried under loans, he realized his quiet choices had given him freedom. The fog had told him he was behind, but he was building resilience. His life wasn't glamorous, but it was steady. And steady was enough.

Cultural Critique: The Algorithm of Achievement

Social media doesn't just show milestones — it amplifies them. It rewards announcements. It hides the ordinary.

You're not comparing lives. You're comparing highlight reels.

The algorithm thrives on urgency: engagements, promotions, graduations, new jobs, new homes. It pushes milestones to the top of your feed, while ordinary days — the ones filled with laundry, doubt, and quiet resilience — disappear.

The result? You compare your full, messy humanity to someone else's curated fragments. And the fog thickens.

Comparison isn't just personal. It's cultural. We live in a system that monetizes milestones, that rewards visibility, that equates speed with success. The fog isn't accidental. It's engineered.

Advertising plays its part too. Every "before and after" photo, every luxury product marketed as proof of arrival, every slogan promising transformation — they all feed the fog. They whisper:

You are behind. You need this to catch up.

Historically, comparison was local. You measured yourself against neighbors, classmates, or colleagues. Today, comparison is global. You measure yourself against thousands of strangers, many of whom you will never meet. The scale is overwhelming, the pace relentless.

This cultural fog convinces us that milestones are the measure of worth. But milestones are fragments, not full lives. They are chapters, not conclusions. And when we forget that, we lose sight of our own compass.

Toolkit: Clearing the Fog

The fog is powerful, but it can be cleared. These practices are designed to help you recognize comparison, reframe it, and reclaim your own pace. Fog Journal

Write down three recent comparison triggers. For each, note:

- What you saw.
- What story the fog told you.
- What truth might be hidden behind the post.

Example:

Trigger: Friend's vacation photo

Fog Story: "She's living her best life, I'm stuck."

Hidden Truth: She may be in debt, stressed, or simply posting one joyful moment.

Reality Check

Ask yourself: What do I actually know? What am I assuming? This separates fact from fog.

Exercise:

- Write down one post that triggered comparison.
- Create two columns: "Known" and "Assumed."

□ Fill them in honestly.

Anchor Values

List five values that matter to you, unrelated to speed or achievement. Examples: kindness, creativity, rest, honesty, presence.

Reflection Prompt: How do these values shift the way you measure your life?

Harbor Exercise

Instead of writing what you want your life to look like, describe what you want it to feel like.

Example:

- Look: Big house, prestigious job, constant travel.
- Feel: Peaceful mornings, meaningful work, time with loved ones.

Fog Break Sentence

Practice saying: “I’m seeing fog, not truth.” Write it three times. Then create your own variation:

- “This is fog, not failure.”
- “Fog distorts, but my compass is steady.”

Comparison Detox Week

Take one week to limit social media. Track how your body feels each day.

Daily Log Example:

- Day 1: Felt restless, kept reaching for my phone.
- Day 3: Noticed more calm in the evening.
- Day 7: Realized I missed fewer moments with my kids.

Highlight Reel Audit

Choose three posts that triggered comparison. Write down what might be missing behind the photo.

Example:

- Post: Engagement photo.
- Missing: Doubt, pressure, financial stress.

Compassionate Mirror Practice

Each morning, write one sentence of compassion to yourself.

Examples:

- "I am allowed to be at my pace."
- "My worth is not measured by milestones."

Slow Pace Rituals

Design one daily ritual that reminds you of your own rhythm. Examples: walking without a destination, cooking slowly, journaling for presence.

Reflection Prompt: How does this ritual anchor you in your own pace?Truth Exchange

Share one hidden truth with a trusted friend. Invite them to share theirs. Notice how fog lifts when masks are removed.

Closing Compass Point

Comparison fog is powerful, but not permanent. It distorts, but it does not define.

When the fog rolls in, remember, you are in your Uncharted Years. Your compass is still there. Your harbor is still there. Your pace is still valid.

Imagine standing at the shoreline after a storm. The fog begins to thin. Slowly, the horizon reappears. You realize the harbor was there all along: steady, waiting, unchanged.

Comparison fog may blur your vision, but it cannot erase your truth.

The fog will lift. And when it does, you'll see you were never lost, just looking in the wrong direction.

Chapter 4

The Pressure to Launch Early

The Unspoken Deadline

There is a deadline no one writes down, but everyone feels. By twenty-five, you're supposed to have a career, a relationship, maybe even a house. By thirty, you're supposed to be settled.

At a birthday dinner, a young woman blew out her candles while relatives asked, "So what's next? Graduate school? Marriage? Kids?" The question wasn't cruel, but it carried weight. She smiled, gave a polite answer, and felt the knot in her stomach tighten. The deadline wasn't on paper, but it was everywhere. It was in conversations, in comparisons, in the silence after she said, "I don't know yet."

The unspoken deadline convinces us that maturity is measured by speed, that milestones prove worth, and that uncertainty is failure. But deadlines belong to projects, not people.

The Countdown Clock

The pressure doesn't just feel like a deadline. It feels like a clock ticking.

A young man lay awake at night, staring at the red glow of his alarm clock. Each birthday felt like another tick forward, another reminder that time was running out. He scrolled through his phone, seeing engagement photos, job announcements, travel posts. The clock wasn't just on his nightstand; it was in his feed, in his head, in his chest.

The fog whispered: You're late. You're behind. You're wasting time.

The countdown clock convinces us that life is a race, that every year is a deadline, that becoming must happen fast. But clocks measure hours, not readiness. The truth is quieter: becoming takes time, and time is not running out.

Why the Pressure Exists

The launch pressure doesn't come from nowhere. It's built from cultural forces that surround young adults every day, whispering urgency and comparison until they feel like they have no choice but to rush.

Productivity Culture

A student sat in the library at 2 a.m., surrounded by empty coffee cups and glowing laptop screens. She whispered to herself, "I can't waste time. I have to keep going." Productivity culture told her that rest was laziness, that slowing down was failure, that worth was measured in output. Achievement Timeline

At graduation, a parent leaned in and said, "Next step:

career, marriage, house." The tassel had barely been moved, yet the timeline was already scripted. The message was clear: adulthood wasn't about becoming; it was about hitting milestones in order, on schedule, without pause.

Social Media Spotlight

At midnight, a young man scrolled through his phone. Engagement photos, job announcements, travel posts; all glowing proof that his peers were "ahead." The glow of the screen became a mirror of comparison. Social media didn't just show lives; it curated illusions of stability and success, amplifying the pressure to perform.

Economic Squeeze

Another young adult sat at the kitchen table, calculator in hand, paycheck in front of her. Rent, groceries, gas; the numbers didn't add up. Survival itself felt urgent.

The economic squeeze convinced her that launching wasn't optional; it was the only way to keep the lights on.

Fear of Falling Behind

And then there was the silence of comparison. Watching peers "launch" while feeling stuck in the harbor. The fear whispered: If you don't move now, you'll be left behind forever.

It wasn't just about milestones. It was about belonging.

The pressure exists because culture confuses speed with success, visibility with stability, milestones with maturity. These forces are loud, constant, and persuasive. They make young adults believe that launching early proves their worth, when in reality it often costs them the very growth they need.

The Academic Launch Pressure

At nineteen, a student declared a major she didn't love because she thought she had to. Everyone around her seemed certain with their choices of engineering, nursing, business, while she still felt undecided. Professors praised her for "getting serious early," but inside she felt trapped. By twenty-one, she was drowning in coursework she hated, convinced she had ruined her future.

The pressure wasn't just internal. At family gatherings, relatives asked, "So what's your major? What's your plan?" Every answer felt like a performance. She smiled, recited her chosen field, and ignored the knot in her stomach. Each semester became another layer of commitment to a path she didn't want, but couldn't admit she had chosen out of fear.

The fog whispered: If you change now, you'll be behind. If you pause, you'll be late. If you explore, you'll fail.

By graduation, she had a degree but no joy. Her diploma felt heavy, not because of pride, but because of the years she had spent silencing herself. Later, she confessed, "I wish someone had told me it was okay not to know yet. I wish someone had said exploration was part of education."

The Academic Launch Pressure convinces students that certainty equals maturity, that speed equals success, that choosing early equals wisdom. But rushing into a major or program before you're ready often leads to foreclosure; the closing off of possibilities before you've even discovered them.

The Girl Who Rushed to Grow Up

There was a girl I knew who rushed into adulthood because she thought that was what being "mature" meant. She moved out at eighteen, signed a lease on a small apartment with peeling paint and second-hand furniture, and took a full-time job that drained her energy before she had even learned how to rest.

Her days blurred together: fluorescent lights at work, microwaved dinners at night, bills stacked on the counter like silent reminders that she was supposed to be grown. Friends posted photos of dorm life, study groups, and late-night adventures, while she sat alone at her kitchen table, staring at overdue notices and wondering if she had made a mistake.

At family gatherings, relatives praised her independence. "You're so responsible," they said. "You've got such a head start." She smiled politely, but inside she felt the weight of exhaustion pressing down. She cried quietly after work, too tired to call anyone, too ashamed to admit she wasn't ready.

The fog whispered: This is adulthood. This is what it means to be mature. If you slow down, you'll fall behind.

She told me later, "I didn't want to grow up. I just didn't want to look like I was falling behind."

Launching early wasn't empowerment; it was fear dressed as maturity. It was a performance of stability that left her lonely, scared, and depleted. Years later, she admitted she wished someone had told her that maturity isn't measured by speed, but by alignment.

The Relationship Launch Pressure

At twenty, a young couple married because they believed adulthood required it. Their families applauded, friends posted photos, and the ceremony looked like a milestone achieved. The reception hall glowed with string lights, the air thick with laughter and clinking glasses. Guests toasted their "maturity," their "stability," their "bright future."

But behind the smiles, both felt overwhelmed. Bills piled up faster than paychecks. Arguments about rent and groceries replaced late-night conversations about dreams. They were still learning who they were as individuals, yet they had already bound themselves together as proof of adulthood.

The fog whispered: Marriage means you're grown. Commitment means you're stable. If you don't do it now, you'll be left behind.

Later, she admitted, "We thought marriage would prove we were adults. But it only proved we were scared of being left behind." He confessed, "I didn't know how to say I wasn't ready.

I thought readiness was something you performed, not something you felt."

Another friend shared a similar story: she rushed into marriage at twenty-three because everyone else was posting engagement photos. "I didn't want to be the last one," she said.

"Now I feel trapped in a commitment I wasn't prepared for."

The Relationship Launch Pressure convinces us that love is a race, that timing is proof of worth, that milestones equal stability. But relationships are not trophies. They are living, breathing commitments that require readiness, honesty, and choice.

Launching early into marriage wasn't maturity. It was fear dressed as stability.

Years later, some of those couples quietly separated, realizing they had rushed into adulthood before they had grown into themselves. Others stayed together but carried the weight of regret, wishing they had been allowed to slow down.

His single status wasn't proof of failure. It was proof of discernment. Proof that waiting for alignment, not rushing for appearances, is the truer form of maturity.

The Cost of Launching Too Soon

Launching early comes with hidden costs. The ones young adults rarely talk about. They don't always show up in photos or posts, but they live in the body, the mind, and the quiet moments no one sees.

Emotional Burnout

One young adult took on a full-time job at twenty while juggling classes. At first, the paycheck felt empowering. But within months, exhaustion became constant. She fell asleep on the bus, cried in the bathroom between shifts, and woke each morning with a knot in her chest. Burnout wasn't a failure of effort — it was the cost of carrying responsibilities her nervous system wasn't ready for.

Identity Foreclosure

Another rushed into a major at nineteen, convinced she had to "decide early." Professors praised her certainty, but inside she felt trapped. By twenty-one, she was drowning in coursework she hated, unable to admit she had chosen out of fear. Her identity had been foreclosed before she had even discovered who she was becoming.

Relationship Pressure

A young couple married at twenty because they believed adulthood required it. Their families applauded, friends posted photos, and the ceremony looked like a milestone achieved. But bills piled up, arguments deepened, and both admitted they had rushed into commitment before they were ready. Stability wasn't alignment. It was pressure disguised as maturity.

Financial Strain

One young man bought a truck and signed a lease right after graduation. His social media looked polished, but debt crept in quietly. Overtime shifts left him drained, and every month felt like a scramble to keep up. Financial strain wasn't proof of independence — it was the hidden cost of launching before he had the skills or support to manage it.

Lost Exploration

Perhaps the most invisible cost is the loss of wandering. A young woman became a parent at twenty-two, skipping the years meant for travel, study, and discovery. She loved her child deeply, but in quiet moments she grieved the paths she hadn't walked. Exploration wasn't wasted time; it was the soil where identity grows.

Launching early isn't always wrong. But launching before you're ready has consequences. Burnout, foreclosure, pressure, strain, and lost exploration are not signs of weakness; they are signs of a culture that confuses speed with success.

The Parenthood Launch Pressure

At twenty-two, a woman became a mother before she felt ready. Social media celebrated her "grown-up life," relatives praised her for "settling down," and she tried to smile through the exhaustion. Her feed filled with congratulatory comments: "You're so mature!" "You've got it all together!" But behind the photos was a body that hadn't yet recovered, a mind that still longed for exploration, and a heart that felt torn between love and loss.

Her days blurred into feedings, laundry, and bills. The apartment smelled faintly of formula and fatigue. Friends posted about internships, travel, and graduate school, while she sat in the quiet of midnight, rocking her baby and wondering if she had skipped the years meant for becoming.

The fog whispered: This is adulthood. This is stability. This is proof you're not behind. Yet she felt both proud and hollow; proud of her child, hollow at the thought of dreams deferred.

Later, she admitted, "I love my child, but I wish I had been allowed to grow up first. I wish someone had told me that readiness isn't about age, it's about alignment." Another young parent confided, "We rushed because everyone else was settling down. But now I feel like I'm raising a child while still raising myself."

The Parenthood Launch Pressure convinces us that maturity is measured by milestones, that having children early proves stability, that family equals readiness. But readiness is not chronological. It is emotional, relational, and deeply personal.

Her early launch into parenthood wasn't failure. It was a collision between cultural timelines and personal readiness. Years later, she realized that what she had lost in exploration, she had gained in resilience. Her child grew, and so did she... slowly, awkwardly, imperfectly. The fog had told her she was behind, but she was simply on a different path, one that required more patience and more grace.

The Night I Felt the Pressure Most

There was a night when I felt the pressure to launch more intensely than ever. I was nineteen, sitting in my car outside my apartment, the dashboard lights casting a dim glow across the steering wheel. The street was quiet, the kind of silence that makes you feel like the world has already moved on without you.

Bills were due. Work was draining. My friends were out living the life I thought I'd have with dorm rooms full of laughter, late-night study sessions, spontaneous road trips. And I was alone, parked in the dark, trying to convince myself that I was okay.

Loneliness pressed in like a weight. I wasn't just tired; I felt lost. I didn't know where I belonged, or if I was even on the right path. The fog whispered: Everyone else is moving forward. You are stuck. You are going nowhere.

In that moment, the pressure narrowed into two options... at least, that's how it felt. Either figure out your life and get on the path everyone expects you to be on. Or get married, and then you'll be adulting correctly. Those were the choices I believed I had. Those were the routes I thought counted. Those were the expectations I had absorbed so deeply that I couldn't tell where they ended and I began.

And I take accountability for that. No one forced those expectations onto me with their hands. I picked them up myself, carried them like weights, and convinced myself they were required for belonging.

I didn't know then that I was allowed to slow down. I didn't know I was allowed to still be becoming. I didn't know I was allowed to choose a different route entirely.

All I knew was that I felt like I had to launch, now, fast, correctly, or I would be left behind. I was trying to launch a rocket with no fuel, sitting alone in the dark, lost in a silence that felt endless.

The Boy Who Launched Too Fast

He graduated high school with a plan, or at least, that's what everyone thought. He went straight into a trade program, then straight into a job, then straight into a relationship that looked stable from the outside. His social media showed him buying a truck, signing a lease, and working overtime. The photos looked like adulthood: steel-toed boots, paychecks, and a life that seemed secure.

But inside, he was unraveling. The smell of grease clung to his clothes after long shifts. His body ached from hours of labor he hadn't yet grown into. He came home late to a quiet apartment, too tired to cook, too drained to talk. His partner praised him for being "responsible," but he felt hollow, as if he was performing a role he hadn't rehearsed.

The fog whispered: You're ahead. You're mature. You're proving yourself. Yet every morning, the alarm clock felt heavier, the drive to work lonelier, the silence louder. He watched his peers still exploring, traveling, studying, experimenting, and felt cut off, as if he had skipped the years meant for becoming.

He told me once, "I didn't know how to say I wasn't ready. I thought readiness was something you performed, not something you felt."

The costs piled up quietly: debt from the truck, strain in his relationship, a creeping sense of isolation. He wasn't failing. He was overwhelmed. He was a young adult trying to live a life that required a version of him he hadn't grown into yet.

Launching early didn't make him mature. It made him tired. It made him lonely. It made him feel lost in a life that looked stable but wasn't aligned. Years later, he admitted that what he needed wasn't speed; it was space. Space to explore, to rest, to grow into himself before carrying the weight of adulthood.

The Career Launch Pressure

At twenty-three, a young man accepted the first stable job offered to him. Everyone congratulated him for "getting ahead." His LinkedIn profile looked polished, his parents proudly told relatives, and his paycheck seemed like proof of success. He bought new work clothes, posted a photo of his office badge, and smiled for the camera.

But every morning, he sat in traffic with a knot in his stomach. The hum of the engine felt heavier than the weight of the commute. By the time he reached the office, fluorescent lights buzzed overhead, emails piled up, and the rhythm of deadlines left him drained. He stared at spreadsheets, wondering if this was what adulthood was supposed to feel like.

His coworkers praised him for being "responsible," but he felt hollow. Friends were still exploring, traveling, studying, experimenting with different paths, while he was locked into a routine that felt more like a cage than a career. The fog whispered: You're secure. You're ahead. You're proving yourself. Yet inside, he felt lost, disconnected from the life he imagined.

The costs piled up quietly: debt from bills he hadn't budgeted for, strain in his relationship as exhaustion replaced joy, and a creeping sense of isolation. He told me once, "I thought I had to lock in a career before twenty-five. Now I feel like I locked myself out of joy."

Launching early into a career didn't make him successful. It made him tired. It made him lonely. It made him feel trapped in a version of adulthood that looked stable but wasn't aligned. Years later, he realized what he needed wasn't speed; it was space. Space to explore, to prepare, to grow into himself before carrying the weight of a career.

The Illusion of Adulthood

We talk about adulthood like it's a switch; one day you're not an adult, and the next day you are. But adulthood is not a moment. It's a slow unfolding.

I remember a young professional who hosted a dinner party in her first apartment. The table was set with mismatched plates, candles flickering, music humming softly in the background. Guests praised her for being "so grown up." She smiled, poured wine, and laughed at the right moments. But inside, she felt like an imposter. The rent was barely paid, the fridge was nearly empty, and she had cried in the bathroom before everyone arrived.

The illusion said: You should know what you're doing. You should feel ready. You should be confident. You should be stable.

Her parents echoed it too: "You're an adult now. You should know better." Friends reinforced it with posts about promotions, engagements, and milestones. The illusion was loud.

But the truth was quieter. Most adults are improvising. Most adults are still becoming. Most adults are still figuring it out.

The cost of the illusion is loneliness. When you believe everyone else has it together, you feel isolated in your uncertainty. You hide your questions, silence your doubts, and pretend you're confident when you're not. The illusion convinces you that struggle is failure, when in reality, struggle is the path.

Adulthood is not a switch. It's a pair of shoes you grow into — slowly, awkwardly, with blisters and adjustments. The illusion is loud. The truth is quiet. And the quiet truth is this: you don't have to launch early to be worthy. You don't have to perform adulthood to belong. You are allowed to still be becoming.

False Urgency: The Engine Behind the Pressure

The launch pressure doesn't just exist; it accelerates. Its engine is false urgency, the cultural hum that insists now is the only acceptable time.

A young adult sat at her desk, scrolling through job postings. Each one seemed to scream: Apply now. Don't wait. Positions filling fast. She felt her chest tighten, convinced that if she didn't act immediately, she would miss her one chance at stability. The urgency wasn't real. Jobs would open again, paths would shift, but the pressure made her believe the window was closing forever.

Another young man stared at his calendar, circling birthdays like deadlines. Twenty-five felt like a cliff, thirty like a verdict. He whispered to himself, "I'm running out of time." The false urgency made him believe adulthood was a race, that every year lost was proof of failure.

False urgency thrives on comparison. It feeds on social media posts, family questions, and cultural scripts. It whispers: If you don't launch now, you'll be left behind. If you pause, you'll never catch up. If you explore, you'll waste time.

But urgency is not the same as readiness. Readiness is alignment: emotional, relational, financial, personal. False urgency confuses speed with success, making young adults believe that rushing is maturity. In reality, rushing often leads to burnout, foreclosure, and regret.

The engine behind the pressure is not truth. It is fear disguised as necessity. And the cost of listening to that engine is losing the quiet space where becoming actually happens.

Cultural Critique: The Myth of Readiness

We are told that adulthood is about readiness; that there comes a moment when you are suddenly prepared, suddenly capable, suddenly mature. But readiness, as culture defines it, is a myth.

A young woman once said, "I thought I'd wake up at twenty-five and feel ready. But I just woke up tired." She had the job, the apartment, the relationship, the milestones. On paper, she was prepared. But inside, she felt like she was improvising every day, still learning who she was, still becoming.

The myth of readiness whispers: You should know by now. You should be confident. You should be stable. It convinces us that uncertainty is failure, that exploration is immaturity, that becoming is something to be hidden.

But readiness is not a switch. It is not a milestone. It is not a moment that arrives with age or achievement. Readiness is alignment. It's the quiet recognition that your choices match your values, that your pace matches your capacity, that your life reflects who you are becoming.

The cultural myth of readiness creates shame. It makes young adults feel behind when they are simply on their own timeline. It silences questions, hides doubts, and forces performances of stability. It tells us that maturity is about certainty, when in truth, maturity is about adaptability.

The critique is this: readiness is not something culture can measure. It is not proven by diplomas, rings, houses, or paychecks. It is lived in the slow unfolding of identity, the patient work of becoming, the courage to admit you are still learning.

The myth is loud. The truth is quieter. And the quiet truth is this: you don't have to be ready to begin. You only have to be willing to grow.

The Truth About Launching

The truth is quieter than the pressure. Launching is not a single moment, not a deadline, not a race. It is a process of becoming: uneven, nonlinear, deeply personal.

A young adult once told me, "I thought launching meant proving I was ready. But it really meant learning how to carry myself while I was still becoming."

The truth is that launching doesn't happen all at once. It happens in small steps: paying a bill, setting a boundary, asking for help, trying again after failure. It happens in pauses as much as in progress.

The truth is that readiness is not measured by age or milestones. It is measured by alignment when your choices match your values, when your pace matches your capacity, when your life reflects who you are becoming.

The truth is that comparison is a thief. Everyone's timeline is different. Some launch into careers early, some into parenthood, some into exploration, some into rest. None of these paths are wrong. They are simply different routes through the same landscape of becoming.

The truth is false urgency is loud, but it is not real. You are not behind. You are not late. You are not failing because you are still learning.

The truth is that launching is not about speed. It is about sustainability. It is about building a life that you can carry, not one that crushes you.

And the deepest truth is this: you are allowed to learn. You are allowed to pause. You are allowed to grow at your own pace.

Launching is not a verdict. It is a journey.

Toolkit: Redefining Readiness

The Launch Pressure Inventory

List all the pressures you feel to launch early.

Circle the ones that aren't yours.

The Readiness Redefinition Write your own definition of readiness.

What does it look like?

What does it feel like?

The Harbor Conditions Check Are you emotionally ready?

Financially ready?

Mentally ready?

Relationally ready?

Spiritually ready?

The Slow Becoming Plan

Write three things you can do to slow down your launch.

Write three things you can do to prepare gently.

The Permission to Pause

Write yourself a note:

"I am allowed to launch at my own pace."

The False Urgency Detector

Write down three decisions you rushed because you felt you

"had to."

What would you choose now, without urgency?

The Illusion Check

List three things you thought adulthood required.

Cross out the ones that were illusions.

Closing Compass Point

You are not late, behind, nor failing. You are becoming. And becoming cannot be rushed. It cannot be forced or timed.

You will launch when your harbor is ready. Not a moment sooner. Not a moment too late.

Your pace is not a problem. It's your path.

Chapter 5

The Emotional Weather of Early Adulthood

The Weather You Don't See Coming

No one warns you that early adulthood comes with weather. We are told to expect decisions, responsibilities, maybe a few detours, but not weather. Not fog thick enough to blur your sense of direction nor storms strong enough to shake your confidence. Not droughts where nothing grows no matter how hard you try. You're not warned of sudden sunbreaks that make everything feel possible again.

We grow up believing adulthood is a map. A map of steps, milestones, and destinations. But it's actually a climate. And like any climate, it shifts, sometimes slowly, sometimes without warning. The problem is cultural silence.

Parents, schools, and workplaces prepare us for tasks and timelines, but not for climates. We are taught how to choose majors, jobs, and partners, but not how to name fog, storms, droughts, or sunbreaks. We are told to measure progress by speed and certainty, not by resilience in changing weather.

So when the climate shifts, most young adults think it's a personal flaw. They think fog means failure, storms mean instability, and drought means laziness. They think sunbreaks mean they've finally "figured it out."

But weather is not identity. It's not character or destiny. Weather is simply what you're moving through. And learning to name your weather is one of the most important skills of the Uncharted Years.

The first weather most young adults encounter is fog; the season of uncertainty.

Fog: The Season of Uncertainty

Fog is the most common weather of early adulthood.

It sounds like:

- "I don't know what I'm doing."
- "I don't know what I want."
- "I don't know where I'm going."

Fog isn't panic or crisis. Fog is the quiet confusion that settles in when you're trying to build a life without a map.

The Fog Years

There was a season in my early twenties when everything felt foggy. It wasn't dramatic or catastrophic. Just unclear.

I would wake up and feel like I was walking through a world where the edges were blurred. I couldn't see more than a few steps ahead or even on the right path. I couldn't tell if I was making progress or just moving in circles.

I didn't know then that fog is a normal part of becoming. I thought it meant I was doing adulthood wrong. But fog is not failure. Fog is simply a lack of visibility; not a lack of worth.

The Friend Who Changed Directions

A friend once told me about a semester when she switched majors twice in three months. Not because she was flaky or indecisive. Because she was in fog.

She would sit in lecture halls and feel like she was watching someone else's life. Everyone else seemed sure and knew what they were doing. What she didn't realize was most of them were pretending. She didn't know that fog was the norm, not the exception.

Fog makes you think you're the only one who can't see. But fog is everywhere. It's just that no one talks about it.

Fog as Failure

Our culture treats uncertainty like a flaw. If you don't know your major, your career, your purpose, your five-year plan, then you're "behind." But fog is not a delay. Fog is a developmental stage. You're not supposed to know everything at nineteen. Or twenty-two. Or twenty-seven. Fog is the space where identity forms.

Reframe: Fog means you're in motion, not lost. And it doesn't last forever.

Sometimes the haze clears just enough for you to see what's ahead and suddenly, everything arrives at once. Responsibilities, deadlines, relationships, bills, expectations. What felt like uncertainty becomes overwhelm.

That's when fog turns into storms.

Storms: The Season of Overwhelm

Storms are the moments when everything hits at once. Bills. Breakups. Deadlines. Family pressure. Identity shifts. Unexpected crises. Fog clears, but instead of clarity, everything arrives at once.

What felt like uncertainty becomes overwhelm. But remember, storms don't mean you're weak. Storms mean you're carrying more than your nervous system was designed to hold at once.

The Week Everything Broke

There was a week when everything fell apart at the same time. My car broke down. My bank account overdrafted. A relationship ended. A job schedule changed without warning.

I remember sitting on the floor, surrounded by laundry and unopened mail, thinking, "Is this what adulthood is supposed to feel like?" It wasn't adulthood. It was a storm.

The Storm of Sudden Responsibility

There was a young man who didn't enter adulthood through milestones; he entered it through responsibility. His mother got sick unexpectedly, and overnight he became the default caretaker for his younger siblings. He was nineteen, still trying to figure out who he was; then suddenly, he was cooking dinners, helping with homework, managing grocery lists, and working part-time to keep the household afloat.

None of these tasks were overwhelming on their own. But together, they formed a storm.

He told me, "I didn't have time to fall apart. I just had to keep going." But inside, he was exhausted. He felt guilty for every moment he wasn't strong, ashamed for every tear he hid, and convinced that struggling meant he was failing.

The storm whispered: This is adulthood. This is what being mature looks like. If you slow down, everything will collapse.

But he wasn't failing. He was carrying more than any nineteen-year-old should have to carry. His storm wasn't instability; it was love under pressure. It was responsibility arriving too soon, too fast, and too heavy.

Years later, he admitted, "I thought my overwhelm meant I wasn't cut out for adulthood. But I was just doing too much, too young, with no support."

His storm wasn't weakness. It was weight. And weight is not a character flaw. Weight is a sign that someone is carrying more than their nervous system was designed to hold.

The Storm of Anger

Another friend described her storm not as collapse, but as rage. She was juggling classes, a job, and family expectations, and one day she snapped. She yelled at people she loved, slammed doors, and cried in her car. She thought her anger meant she was broken.

But it was just another kind of storm; the nervous system overflowing when too much arrives at once.

Storm Shame

Storms are often invisible. You can be drowning and still show up to work. You can be overwhelmed and still post a smiling photo. You can be falling apart and still look "fine."

Our culture glorifies resilience without support. It praises "handling it all" as if breaking is weakness.

But storms are not meant to be weathered alone.

Reframe: Storms are not proof you're failing. They're proof you're human. Storms DO NOT last forever.

But sometimes, after the chaos quiets, you don't feel relief; you feel emptiness. The rain stops, the noise fades, and instead of clarity, there's silence. That silence is drought.

Drought: The Season of Numbness

Drought is the quietest weather and often the most misunderstood. It's the season when you feel disconnected, unmotivated, flat, like nothing is growing.

Drought isn't laziness; it's depletion.

It happens when you've been in survival mode for too long. When you've been hustling without rest. When you've been performing adulthood instead of living it.

There was a year when I couldn't feel much of anything. Not joy. Not excitement. Not sadness. I wasn't depressed or broken.

I was empty.

I had been giving and giving and giving emotionally, financially, relationally, without replenishment. Drought is what happens when you run out of yourself.

A friend once told me, "I don't feel anything anymore. I just go through the motions." She woke up, went to work, came home, scrolled her phone, and went to bed. Her life looked fine from the outside; bills paid, responsibilities met, milestones checked. But inside, she felt flat. She wasn't lazy. She was in drought. Her body had shifted into conservation mode, protecting her from further depletion.

Our culture rewards burnout. It praises productivity and glorifies exhaustion. So when drought hits, young adults blame themselves. They think they're unmotivated and lazy. They think they're falling behind.

But drought is not a moral failure. It's a biological response to depletion.

Reframe: Drought is not a character flaw. It's a sign you need replenishment, not discipline. Drought DOES NOT last forever.

Even in the quietest seasons, small sparks eventually return. A conversation, a morning, a breath; these are reminders that clarity can break through.

That's the gift of sunbreaks.

Sunbreaks: The Season of Clarity

Sunbreaks are the moments when everything suddenly makes sense. A conversation. A realization. A moment of peace. A small win. A breath that feels different.

Sunbreaks don't last forever, either, but they don't need to. They give you just enough clarity to keep going.

I remember the first time I felt a sunbreak after years of fog and storms. It wasn't a dramatic or life-changing moment.

It was a quiet morning. I was sitting at my kitchen table, drinking coffee, and for the first time in a long time, I felt... okay. The fog lifted just enough for me to see a few steps ahead. So, I sat with it and embraced the feeling. The storm quieted just enough for me to breathe. The drought eased just enough for me to feel a spark of possibility.

That's what sunbreaks do. They don't fix everything, but they remind you that everything can change.

A friend once told me her sunbreak came on a bus ride home. She was staring out the window, exhausted from work, when she suddenly noticed the sky turning pink. For the first time in weeks, she felt a flicker of calm. Nothing in her circumstances had changed; the bills were still waiting, the deadlines still looming, but something inside shifted. That's what sunbreaks do. They remind you that clarity can arrive in ordinary moments.

Reframe: Sunbreaks are not the end of the journey. They're the encouragement along the way.

Microclimates: The Weather Inside the Weather

Sometimes your emotional weather doesn't match your external life.

You can be in:

- A storm at work but a sunbreak in your friendships
- A drought in your identity but clarity in your goals
- Fog in your relationships but stability in your finances

A student once told me, "My life feels split in half." At school, she was in fog; unsure of her major, uncertain about her future, pretending to be confident while feeling lost. But in her friendships, she was in a sunbreak. She was laughing, belonging, and feeling seen. She thought the contradiction meant she was unstable. But she wasn't unstable. She was layered. She was living inside microclimates.

A young professional once told me she felt storm every time she opened her bank app; panic, pressure, fear. But in her creative life, she was in a sunbreak. She painted at night, shared her work with friends, and felt alive. She thought the contradiction meant she was off-track. But it simply meant she was living inside microclimates; storm in one part of life, sunbreak in another.

Naming those microclimates helped her realize that she wasn't broken. She was just navigating different emotional weathers in different parts of her life.

The Weather Forecast Myth

Adults love to pretend they can forecast emotional weather. Funny, considering most of them still get the real forecast wrong.

They say things like:

- "You'll understand when you're older."
- "You'll know when it's time."
- "You'll feel ready."

But emotional weather doesn't follow logic. It doesn't follow age or timelines. You can't forecast emotional weather with precision. You can only prepare for it.

The myth of the forecast creates shame. It makes young adults think they should have seen things coming.

It makes them think they should have known better or should have been prepared for the unknown.

A young adult once told me she thought she should have

"seen it coming." Relatives had reassured her that she would "just know" when it was time to choose a career, but when graduation arrived, she felt nothing but panic. She blamed herself for not feeling ready, for not predicting the fog that settled in. Later she realized the problem wasn't her; it was the myth of the forecast. She hadn't failed. She had just encountered weather that no one can predict.

But you can't predict these things. You can't predict fog, storms, droughts, or sunbreaks. You can only learn to navigate them.

Toolkit: Emotional Weather Mapping

Identify Your Current Weather

Circle one: Fog • Storm • Drought • Sunbreak

Describe the Conditions

What does this weather feel like in your body?

In your mind?

In your relationships?

Map Your Triggers

What tends to bring on this weather?

What tends to intensify it?

Build Your Storm Shelter

List three things that help ground you when you're feeling overwhelmed.

Create Your Sunbreak Anchors

List three things that reliably bring you small moments of clarity or peace.

Track Your Patterns

Over the next week, note your emotional weather each day.

What patterns emerge?

Write Your Weather Permission Slip

- "I am allowed to be in fog."
- "I am allowed to be in drought."
- "I am allowed to be in storms."
- "I am allowed to enjoy sunbreaks without waiting for the other shoe to drop."

Microclimate Mapping Where are you in fog?

Where are you in sunbreak?

Where are you in drought?

Where are you in storm?

The Weather Conversation

Share your weather with someone you trust. Let them share theirs. Notice how normal it feels. Closing Compass Point

Weather changes and so do you. Fog lifts. Storms pass.

Droughts end. Sunbreaks return.

Your emotional weather is not a verdict, not a diagnosis, and definitely not a measure of your worth. It's simply the climate of becoming. And you are learning to navigate it with more clarity, compassion, and courage than you realize.

Chapter 6

The Identity Earthquake

When the Ground Beneath You Shifts

There comes a moment in early adulthood when the ground beneath you moves. Not physically; not dramatically. But internally, in a way you can't ignore. It's the moment you realize the identity you've been carrying isn't yours anymore. Or maybe it never was.

It's the moment when:

- The roles you've been performing stop fitting
- The expectations you've been following stop making sense
- The version of yourself you've been presenting stops feeling true

It's not destruction, it's disruption. A necessary cracking so something truer can emerge. It happens in tremors, small cracks, and quiet doubts. There are moments of discomfort that accumulate until something finally breaks open. When it does, it can feel terrifying.

It can also feel like the beginning of freedom. I remember the first time I felt the ground shift beneath me. It wasn't a crisis or a breakdown. It was a quiet moment; the kind that doesn't look like anything from the outside. I was sitting in a room full of people who seemed so sure of themselves. They talked about their plans, their goals, their five-year trajectories. They spoke with confidence, certainty, and direction. All I felt was misaligned. I wasn't jealous or intimidated. I was aware that the version of myself I was performing didn't match the version of myself I was becoming. It was the first crack in the identity I had been carrying.

But it was enough to make me wonder:

- Who am I when I'm not performing?
- Who am I when I'm not pleasing?
- Who am I when I'm not trying to be what everyone expects?

That was the beginning of the earthquake.

Why Identity Shakes in Early Adulthood

Identity doesn't collapse because you're unstable. It collapses because you're growing. Several forces make early adulthood a prime time for identity earthquakes:

The Collapse of Childhood Roles

You're no longer the student, the child, the dependent, the one being guided. Those roles fall away, and you're left with space you don't know how to fill.

The Pressure to Define Yourself Too Early

You're asked to choose a major, a career, a path, or a partner before you've had time to explore who you are.

The Disillusionment of Performed Identity

You realize the identity you've been presenting was built for approval, not authenticity.

The Emergence of Your Inner Voice

For the first time, you can hear your own desires, and they don't always match the expectations you were raised with.

The Emotional Weather of Becoming

Fog, storms, droughts, and sunbreaks all destabilize the old identity and make space for a new one.

Identity earthquakes aren't failures. They're awakenings.

There was a version of me that tried so hard to be "the good one." The responsible and mature one. The version who didn't cause trouble and made the "right" choices. Being the "good one" teaches you how to perform, not how to belong.

I remember sitting in a job interview, smiling politely, answering every question with what I thought was the "right" response. The interviewer nodded, impressed. On paper, I looked great. Inside, I felt hollow. I realized I was performing a version of myself that no longer fit; a version built for applause, not alignment.

I didn't realize I had outgrown that identity until I found myself living a life that didn't feel like mine. It was a life built on expectations, not authenticity; on performance, not truth.

The earthquake didn't destroy me, but it did the version of me that wasn't real.

She was twenty-three when she realized she didn't recognize the person in her own life. She had the job she thought she wanted. She had the relationship she thought she was supposed to have. She had the apartment, the routine, the responsibilities.

But she didn't have herself.

One evening, she stood in front of her bathroom mirror, toothbrush in hand, staring at her reflection. The face looking back seemed familiar but foreign; polished enough to pass, tired enough to betray her. She whispered, "I don't know who you are anymore."

She told me, “I built a life that looked right from the outside, but I don’t fit inside it.”

That’s the identity earthquake; the moment you realize the life you’re living doesn’t match the person you’re becoming.

The Roles We Wear Without Knowing

Most young adults don’t realize they’re performing an identity until it starts to crack.

You perform the role of:

- The achiever
- The caretaker
- The responsible one
- The funny one
- The strong one
- The agreeable one
- The one who “has it together”

These roles aren’t lies; they’re adaptations. You learned them to survive and belong. You performed them to be loved, to avoid conflict, and to meet expectations.

But performed identity has a shelf life. Eventually, the real you starts pushing against the walls, and that pressure is the beginning of the earthquake.

Mourning the Person You Thought You'd Be

Identity earthquakes don't just shake you; they break your heart a little. This is because you're not just losing an identity.

You're losing:

- A dream
- A plan
- A version of yourself you invested in
- A story you thought you'd live
- A future you imagined

Identity grief is real. It's the ache of realizing you've outgrown a future you once loved. It's the sadness that comes when you realize the person you thought you'd be isn't the person you're becoming.

I remember sitting on the floor surrounded by old journals, reading the dreams I once wrote down. Careers, relationships, and milestones are all mapped out for a version of me I had already outgrown. The grief wasn't just about losing those plans.

It was about realizing they belonged to someone I no longer was.

You're not failing. You're evolving. But please know, evolution has grief in it.

The Identity I Had to Let Go Of

There was a version of me I held onto long after she stopped fitting. She was composed and predictable. She was what I thought adulthood required.

Letting her go felt like betrayal; like I was disappointing the people who believed in her.

I remember the day I stopped waking up at 5:30 a.m. to "get ahead." It seems small, but for me it was seismic. I had built an identity around discipline because I thought adulthood demanded it. Early alarms, rigid routines, productivity before sunrise; all part of the performance. One morning, I let myself sleep in. I felt no guilt or looming punishment; no self-lecture about falling behind. The world didn't collapse. No one noticed. But inside, I felt the crack widen.

She wasn't me. She was the version of me I created to survive a life I no longer lived. Grieving her was honest; not weakness.

Who You Become After the Earthquake

After the ground shakes, there's a moment of stillness. A moment when you look around at the pieces of your old identity and wonder what to do with them.

This is the reconstruction phase, the slow, intentional rebuilding of who you are. Reconstruction is not glamorous, linear, or quick.

It looks like:

- Trying new things
- Saying no more often
- Saying yes more honestly
- Letting yourself be seen
- Letting yourself be wrong
- Letting yourself change

Reconstruction is the quiet work of becoming. It's the part no one applauds, but it's where the real self begins to take shape. It's like the slow clearing after a storm. It's not instant, but steady. Each small act of alignment is a sunbreak that reminds you rebuilding is possible.

The Boy Who Rebuilt Slowly

He told me, "I thought the earthquake meant I was broken. But it was the first time I had space to figure out who I actually was." He rebuilt slowly. He left a career that didn't fit and ended a relationship that wasn't aligned. He moved to a new city, tried new hobbies, and made friends who knew the real him.

I remember him describing the first time he picked up a guitar. His fingers stumbled over the strings, clumsy and uncertain, but he felt alive. For the first time in years, he wasn't performing for approval; he was experimenting for himself. That small act of trying something new became a symbol of his reconstruction. He didn't rebuild the old identity. He built a truer one.

Toolkit: Navigating the Identity Earthquake

You don't need to rebuild your identity all at once. Here are practices to help you navigate your own identity earthquake, not assignments, but invitations.

The Identity Audit

Write down the roles you've been performing.

Circle the ones that no longer fit.

The Inner Voice Check

What desires have been whispering beneath the noise?

What have you been afraid to admit you want?

The Earthquake Map

List the moments that shook your sense of self.

What were they trying to reveal?

The Permission to Evolve Write:

"I am allowed to outgrow versions of myself that no longer fit."

The Alignment Test

For each major decision, ask:

"Is this choice coming from expectation or authenticity?"

The Identity Debris List

What beliefs, expectations, or roles fell away during your earthquake?

What did their collapse make space for?

The Becoming Statement

Write a sentence that begins with:

"I am becoming someone who..."

Let it be honest.

The Reconstruction Plan

List three small steps toward the identity you're growing into.

The Identity Anchor

Choose one value that feels true to who you're becoming. Let it guide your next season.

You don't have to do them all. Choose the practices that feel gentle and true for you.

Closing Compass Point

Identity is not a destination; it's a landscape that shifts as you do. It shifts and cracks. It reshapes itself. You are not failing or behind because you're changing and evolving. You are not lost because the ground is moving. You are becoming and becoming is not supposed to feel stable. It's supposed to feel true.

Like weather, identity shifts are meant to move. Fog clears, storms pass, droughts ease, sunbreaks arrive, and each shift makes space for becoming.

Chapter 7

The Quiet Rebuild

The Stillness After the Shaking

No one tells you that the aftermath of an identity earthquake isn't clarity. It's quiet. Not peace nor certainty. Just quiet. The kind of quiet that feels unfamiliar at first. The quiet that makes you aware of how loud your life used to be; the expectations, the roles, the pressure, the performance.

After the shaking stops, there's a moment when everything feels suspended. You're not who you were. You're not yet who you're becoming. You're somewhere in between.

This in between is the beginning of the rebuild. And rebuilds don't start with action. They start with stillness.

There was a morning, not tied to any dramatic event or marked by any milestone, when I woke up and felt... different. Not healed. Not transformed. Just aware that something inside me had shifted.

I made coffee and sat at the kitchen table. Then, for the first time in a long time, I didn't feel the urge to perform. I didn't feel the need to prove anything or the pressure to be impressive.

It wasn't clarity. It was quiet. And that quiet felt like the first brick of a new foundation.

The Nature of Quiet Work

Rebuilding identity is not loud work. It's not dramatic. It's not something you can post about or measure or show off.

Quiet work is:

- Slow
- Subtle
- Nonlinear
- Often invisible to others
- Often misunderstood as "doing nothing" But quiet work is the most important work of becoming.

It's the work of:

- Listening to yourself
- Honoring your needs
- Letting go of old roles
- Choosing new truths
- Relearning how to trust your own voice

Quiet work is where identity grows; slowly, invisibly, and with more strength than you expect.

The Three Phases of the Quiet Rebuild

Every rebuild moves through three phases. It moves in a rhythm.

Phase 1: Clearing the Rubble

Before you can rebuild, you have to clear what collapsed. This phase is messy, emotional, and very uncomfortable.

Clearing the rubble looks like:

- Letting go of old beliefs
- Releasing roles that no longer fit
- Ending relationships that were built on performance
- Questioning the stories you were raised with
- Admitting what's not working

It's the phase when you realize how much of your life was built on expectations instead of alignment.

There was a day when I realized I couldn't keep pretending to be the version of myself everyone expected. I didn't make a dramatic change. I simply stopped performing. I stopped saying yes when I meant no, and stopped being so agreeable to things that drained me. I stopped trying to be the "good one" or the "nice one," roles that had earned me approval but cost me authenticity.

Clearing the rubble wasn't glamorous. It was honest. Our culture tells you that clearing is wasteful. That letting go is failure and stopping is quitting.

But clearing is not quitting. Clearing is choosing.

Reframe:

Clearing the rubble is not destruction. It's preparation.

Phase 2: Laying the Foundation

Once the rubble is cleared, there's space, and space can feel terrifying. This is the phase where you choose what your new identity will rest on.

Foundations are built from:

- Values
- Boundaries
- Truths
- Desires
- Needs
- Self knowledge

This phase is slow, reflective, and deeply internal.

I decided I wanted a life that felt quiet, grounded, and uncluttered; internally and externally. I remember the first time I chose to use a boundary that my brother taught me. He told me that he never does more than what his emotional bandwidth can handle.

I began practicing, and it was easier than I thought it would be. I was very honest with myself and measured everything according to what my emotional bandwidth could manage and wanted to manage.

Choosing that boundary changed everything. It became the foundation I built the next version of myself around. Anything that felt "too much" was set aside until I was ready. For the first time, my capacity became the measure. It no longer came from expectations, pressure, or performance. I was protecting my peace and finding what aligned with me.

Reframe:

You don't build your foundation from expectations. You build it from alignment.

Phase 3: Building the New Rooms

This is the phase where you begin to explore the new version of yourself. It's experimental, playful, and gentle.

Building the new rooms looks like:

- Trying new hobbies
- Forming new friendships
- Setting new boundaries
- Speaking up differently

- Dressing differently
- Choosing differently
- Dreaming differently

This phase is where you realize you're not rebuilding the old identity; you're building a truer one.

The first "room" I built in my new identity was creativity. It was writing, naming emotional truths, and building frameworks that helped people feel less alone. That room became a home.

Reinvention is often portrayed as dramatic: a big move, a big change, a big announcement. Real reinvention is quiet and subtle. It's the accumulation of small, aligned choices.

Reframe:

Reinventing yourself doesn't happen in one moment. It takes a thousand small ones.

The Slow Return to Self

A client of mine told me about her journey. She didn't rebuild her life overnight. She rebuilt it slowly and cleared the rubble by ending a relationship that no longer fit. She laid the foundation by choosing values that felt true. She built new rooms by trying things she had always been curious about but never allowed herself to explore. Returning to yourself is the quietest kind of victory, and the most profound.

The Myth of the Overnight Transformation

Transformation is often portrayed as sudden or like a breakthrough. It's portrayed as a revelation; a moment of clarity. But real transformation is slow and quiet. It's progress.

It happens in:

- Small decisions
- Tiny shifts
- Quiet realizations
- Subtle changes
- Daily choices

The myth of the overnight transformation creates shame. It convinces people that slow growth is failure, when in reality it's the most sustainable kind. It makes young adults think they're behind or not changing fast enough. No one's rebuild is too slow. Slow is honest and real.

The Daily Ritual

Another young adult told me her rebuild began with something small: making tea every evening. She cleared the rubble by letting go of the pressure to be productive at night. She laid her foundation by choosing rest as a value. She built new rooms by turning that tea ritual into a space for journaling, reflection, and quiet joy. It wasn't dramatic. It was daily. Daily choices are the bricks of reconstruction.

Toolkit: The Quiet Rebuild Guide

Identify What Needs Clearing

List the beliefs, roles, or expectations that no longer fit.

Choose Your Foundation Values

Pick three values that feel true to who you're becoming.

Name Your New Boundaries

Write one boundary you're ready to set, even if it's small.

Create a "Small Steps" Plan

List three tiny actions that move you toward alignment.

Track Your Emotional Energy

Notice what drains you and what replenishes you.

Celebrate Micro Growth

Write down one small shift you made this week.

Build One New Room

Choose one area of your life to explore gently: creativity, rest, connection, curiosity. You don't have to do them all. Choose the practices that feel gentle and true for you.

Closing Compass Point

Rebuilding doesn't need to be loud to be real. It doesn't need to be fast to be meaningful. It doesn't need to be impressive to be transformative.

You are rebuilding quietly, honestly, and in alignment with who you are becoming.

Quiet rebuilds are like sunbreaks after storms; subtle, steady, and enough to remind you that becoming is possible.

Chapter 8

The Slow Becoming

Becoming is a Pace

There's a myth that becoming is like a revelation. A breakthrough. A moment of clarity that changes everything. But becoming is not a moment. It's a pace. It's the slow, steady unfolding of who you are when you stop performing and start listening. It's the quiet shift that happens after the earthquake, after the rebuild, after the dust settles.

Becoming is not dramatic. It's not something you can point to and say, "There. That's when it happened." Becoming is subtle, but still growth. It's the kind of growth you only notice in hindsight; the kind that accumulates quietly until it becomes undeniable. It's the result of a thousand small choices that slowly align you with yourself. You don't wake up one day as a new person. You wake up one day and realize you've been becoming for a long time.

The First Time I Noticed I Was Different

There was a small moment when I realized I was responding differently. Someone asked me to do something I didn't have the capacity for. The old me would have said yes immediately and rearranged my life to make it work. The old me would have dealt with the discomfort and the annoyance at myself for saying yes.

But this time, I paused and checked in with myself; checked my emotional bandwidth. And I said, "I can't do that today." It was such a strange feeling. It wasn't a big deal to them, but to me, it was everything.

It was the first time I realized I was becoming someone who honored her own limits. Becoming doesn't announce itself. It reveals itself.

The Myth of the "New You"

Reinvention culture loves the idea of the "new you." A sudden transformation or a dramatic shift. A before-and-after reveal.

But that's not how real becoming works.

Real becoming is:

- gradual
- nonlinear
- quiet
- internal
- often invisible until you look back

It doesn't erase who you were; it reveals who you've been growing into. You don't become someone new. You become someone true. The myth of the "new you" creates pressure. This can make young adults think they need to reinvent themselves overnight. They may think they're behind if they're not changing fast enough. But becoming is rarely obvious. It's felt before it's seen.

The Three Layers of Becoming

Becoming happens in layers: internal, external, and integrated. You move through them slowly, often without realizing it.

Layer 1: Internal Shifts This is the layer no one sees.

It's the quiet work of:

- questioning old beliefs
- choosing new values
- listening to your desires

noticing what feels aligned

setting boundaries internally before you set them

externally

Internal shifts are subtle. They're the whispers before the words. The nudges before the decisions. The knowing before the action.

I remember sitting alone one night, thinking about a decision I needed to make. The old me would have asked, "What will people think?" But this time, the question that surfaced was, "What feels right for me?"

It startled me and felt unfamiliar. But it felt true in a way I couldn't ignore. That was the beginning of my internal becoming.

Reframe:

Internal shifts are not indecision. They're the foundation of alignment.

Layer 2: External Expressions

This is the layer where becoming becomes visible.

It looks like:

- changing habits
- setting boundaries
- choosing different relationships
- dressing differently
- speaking differently
- making decisions from alignment instead of fear

External expressions are the behaviors that grow from your internal shifts. The first external change I made was tiny: I rearranged my space. I cleared out things that didn't feel like me anymore and made room for things that did.

It wasn't about décor, but about identity. It was the first time my outer world reflected my inner one.

Reframe:

External changes don't make you who you are. They reflect who you're becoming.

Layer 3: Identity Integration

This is the layer where the internal and external finally match. It's not a moment. It's a feeling.

Integration feels like:

- ease
- clarity
- self-trust

alignment relief

It's the moment when you realize you're no longer performing. You're simply being.

There was a day when I decided without overthinking it. I didn't ask permission. I didn't worry about approval. I trusted myself.

Did I believe I had all the answers? Of course not. However, I did finally believe I could handle whatever came next. That was integration. It was alignment.

I remember standing at my kitchen counter, choosing what to cook for dinner. It sounds ordinary, but for years I had chosen meals based on what others wanted or what seemed "right." That night, I chose what felt nourishing to me. No hesitation. No second-guessing. Just ease. That's what integration feels like. It feels like the quiet confidence of living in alignment even in the smallest choices.

Reframe:

Integration is not the end of becoming. It's the beginning of living.

The Person Who Didn't Realize They'd Changed

He didn't think he had changed. He still felt uncertain, still felt messy, still felt like he was figuring things out. But then one day, he ran into someone from his past, someone who knew the old version of him.

They talked for a few minutes, and afterward he realized a few things. He didn't react the way he used to. He didn't shrink, perform, or pretend. He was calm and grounded. He was himself.

He hadn't reinvented himself. He had become himself. And becoming yourself is the quietest kind of transformation with no need for an announcement.

The conversation had taken place in a coffee shop, with the hum of voices and clinking cups. It wasn't dramatic or staged. It was ordinary. And that ordinariness made the realization even more powerful. He had changed so quietly that he hadn't noticed until someone else gave him a chance to notice.

The Compass You Build Along the Way

Becoming doesn't give you a map. It gives you a compass. A map tells you where to go. A compass guides you.

Your compass is built from:

- your values

your boundaries your desires

- your lived experience
- your emotional weather
- your identity reconstruction

It doesn't give you certainty. It gives you orientation, and orientation is enough. Your compass steadies you even when the weather shifts through fog, storms, or sunbreaks.

The First Time I Trusted My Own Direction

There was a moment when I had to make a choice; one that didn't make sense to anyone else. The old me would have polled everyone I knew. I would have gathered opinions, weighed expectations, tried to choose the "right" thing. But this time, I didn't ask anyone. I listened to myself. And I chose the direction that felt aligned, even though it wasn't the obvious one. It wasn't confidence. It was trust. Trust is quieter than confidence, but far more powerful. That's what becoming gives you: not certainty, but trust.

Toolkit: The Slow Becoming Practices

Track Your Micro-Shifts

Write down one small way you responded differently this week.

Identify Your New Patterns

What choices feel more aligned than they used to?

Notice What Feels True

Pay attention to the moments when your body says yes or no.

Practice Self-Led Decisions

Make one decision this week without asking for external validation.

Build Your Compass Statements

Write three statements that begin with:

"I'm becoming someone who..."

Celebrate Subtle Growth

Name one quiet change you're proud of.

You don't have to practice them all. Choose the ones that feel aligned with your pace.

Closing Compass Point

Becoming is not something you force. It's something you allow. It's slow, gentle, honest, and yours.

You are not behind, late, or lost. You are becoming, and you're doing it at your own pace, in your own rhythm, in your own time.

Becoming doesn't need to be seen to be real. It unfolds quietly, and that quiet is its strength. Becoming is not measured by speed. It's measured by honesty.

Chapter 9

The Compass You Build

You Don't Need a Map When You Have a Compass

Maps are comforting because they promise certainty and clarity. They promise a straight line from here to there.

But maps only work when the terrain is known, and early adulthood is not known terrain. It's shifting, unpredictable, nonlinear. It's packed full of detours, false starts, unexpected turns, and seasons you never saw coming.

A map can't help you here, but a compass can. A compass doesn't tell you where to go. It tells you what direction feels true.

And that's what you've been building; your compass. Not all at once, but slowly through every aligned choice you've made.

Your compass is made of:

- your values

- your boundaries
- your emotional weather
- your identity shifts
- your lived experience
- your self-trust
- your alignment

It's not perfect or precise. It's not meant to be. It's meant to guide you, not control you.

The First Time I Realized I Had a Compass

There was a moment years after the fog, the storms, the pressure, the earthquake, the rebuild, when I realized I wasn't lost anymore. Not because I had everything figured out or because my life was perfect. I had no plan, but I had a direction.

I was making choices from alignment, not fear. I was listening to myself instead of performing for others. I was moving toward what felt true instead of what looked right. I didn't have a map, but I had a compass, and that was enough.

What a Compass Actually Does

A compass doesn't eliminate uncertainty or prevent detours.

And it definitely doesn't guarantee ease.

A compass does one thing: It keeps you oriented toward yourself.

It helps you:

- choose the next right step
- recognize when something feels off
- notice when you're drifting from your values
- return to alignment
- trust your own pace
- trust your own voice

A compass doesn't make the journey easier. It makes it yours.

And yours is enough even when the pat is unclear.

The Four Directions of Your Compass

Every compass has four directions, yours included. The directions are not north, south, east, west; but something deeper.

North: Your Values - The truths you choose to live by. Not inherited or expected. Chosen.

South: Your Boundaries - The lines that protect your energy, your peace, your becoming.

East: Your Desires - The things that pull you forward; quietly, consistently, honestly.

West: Your Self-Trust - The belief that you can handle what comes next, even without a map.

When these four directions align, you don't feel lost even when you don't know where you're going.

The Person Who Finally Trusted Their Compass

She spent years trying to follow the "right" path. The path everyone said would lead to success, stability, belonging. It just never felt like hers.

After her identity earthquake, after her quiet rebuild, after her slow becoming, she started making decisions differently.

She didn't ask, "What should I do?" Instead she asked, "What feels aligned?"

She didn't ask, "What will people think?" She asked, "What do I think?"

She didn't ask, "What's the right route?" She asked, "What direction feels true?"

And slowly, her life began to feel like her own. She wasn't following a map. She was following her compass. For the first time, her life felt like it belonged to her.

The Compass Is Internal, Not External

No one else can build your compass but you. Not your parents, friends, or professors. Not your partner or society. Your compass is internal. It's built from your lived experience, your emotional truth, your becoming. And because it's internal, no one else can override it.

People can give advice, offer perspective, and hand you their maps. But only you can feel your direction.

The First Time I Said "This Is My Direction"

There was a moment when someone questioned a choice I made. It was a choice that didn't make sense to them.

The old me would have explained, justified, maybe even apologized. But this time, I just responded with, "This is my direction." I wasn't defensive or angry. Just clear.

I wasn't asking for permission or seeking approval. I wasn't trying to be understood; I was trying to be aligned. I was following my compass, and that clarity felt like freedom.

The Compass Doesn't Prevent Detours, It Helps You

Navigate Them

Detours are part of the journey. So are pauses and setbacks.

So are seasons of fog, storms, drought, and sunbreaks.

Your compass doesn't eliminate these seasons. It helps you move through them without losing yourself.

It helps you:

- stay grounded in fog
- stay steady in storms
- stay gentle in drought
- stay open in sunbreaks

Your compass doesn't promise ease; it promises orientation.

Toolkit: Building and Trusting Your Compass

Identify Your True North (Values)

Write down three values that feel aligned with who you're becoming.

Define Your South (Boundaries)

List two boundaries that protect your energy and your becoming.

Name Your East (Desires) What pulls you forward?

What feels like possibility?

Strengthen Your West (Self-Trust)

Write one moment when you trusted yourself — even a small one.

Compass Check-In

Ask yourself:

"Does this choice move me toward or away from myself?"

The Alignment Test

If a decision feels heavy, it's misaligned.

If it feels grounded, it's true.

The Compass Statement

Write:

"I don't need a map. I have a compass."

You don't have to practice them all. Choose the ones that feel aligned with your needs.

Closing Compass Point

You were never meant to have a map. You were meant to have a compass. A map would have trapped you in someone else's route. A compass frees you to follow your own.

You are not behind, late, or lost. You are becoming, rebuilding, and navigating. And you are doing it with a compass built from your own truth.

This is not the end of your journey. It's the beginning of your direction. Your compass doesn't need to be perfect. It only needs to be yours, and yours is enough to carry you through every season of becoming.

Conclusion

Conclusion

There will come a moment - maybe soon, maybe quietly, maybe without fanfare - when you realize you're no longer waiting for someone to hand you a map.

You're no longer trying to catch up or measuring yourself against timelines that were never meant for you.

You're no longer searching for the version of you that other people expected. You're simply here... in your own life, your own pace, your own becoming. Presence becomes your anchor, not performance.

The uncharted years don't end with certainty. They end with orientation - a sense of direction that comes from within, not from the world around you.

You won't always know the next step or feel confident. You also won't always move forward in a straight line. But you will know yourself, which is the most important. And that knowing will guide you more faithfully than any map ever could.

You don't need to see the whole path to trust the step you are taking. As you step into whatever comes next, remember this:

You are not behind.

You are not late.

You are not lost.

You are becoming: slowly, honestly, and in your own time.

And that is enough.

Epilogue

If you reached this page and you're feeling overwhelmed, hopeless, or unsure how to keep going, I want you to know this clearly:

You are not alone. You are not failing. You are not a burden. You are not beyond help.

The uncharted years can feel heavy. They can feel confusing. They can feel like too much. If you're in a season where everything feels dark or impossible, please reach out to someone who can sit with you in it.

Talk to someone you trust, whether it's a friend, a family member, a mentor, or a therapist. You don't have to explain everything perfectly. You don't have to be strong. You just have to reach out.

And if you need immediate support, you can call or text 988 for the Suicide & Crisis Lifeline. It's available 24/7. It's free. It's confidential. You don't have to be in crisis to reach out; you can call simply because you need someone to talk to.

Asking for help is not weakness. It's courage. It's connection.

It's human.

You are not behind. You are not late. You are not lost. You are needed. You are worthy. You are becoming, even if today feels heavy.

If you're struggling, please stay. Reach out. Let someone walk with you. Your story is still unfolding, and the world is better with you in it.

www.ingramcontent.com/pod-product-compliance
Lightning Source LLC
LaVergne TN
LVHW100147061126
851857LV00010B/284
* 9 7 9 8 9 0 6 5 6 0 0 1 8 *